GREAT DISASTERS

THE ATTACK ON THE LUSITANIA

RUPERT MATTHEWS

Illustrated by
Nik Spender

The Bookwright Press
New York · 1989

Great Disasters

The Black Death
The Chernobyl Catastrophe
The Hindenburg Tragedy
The Eruption of Krakatoa
The Fire of London

The Attack on the Lusitania
The Destruction of Pompeii
The San Francisco Earthquake
The Space Shuttle Disaster
The Sinking of the Titanic

First published in the
United States in 1989 by
The Bookwright Press
387 Park Avenue South
New York, NY 10016

First published in 1989 by
Wayland (Publishers) Limited
61 Western Road, Hove
East Sussex BN3 1JD, England

Library of Congress Cataloging-in-Publication Data
Matthews, Rupert.
  The attack on the Lusitania / by Rupert Matthews; [illustrated by Nik Spender].
    p.   cm.—(Great disasters)
  Bibliography: p.
  Includes index.
  Summary: An account of the attack and sinking of the passenger liner, the Lusitania, by the German torpedo during World War I.
    ISBN 0-531-18286-X
  1. Lusitania (Steamship)—Juvenile literature. [1. Lusitania (Steamship)] I. Spender, Nik, ill.   II. Title.   III. Series.
D592.L8M38   1989
940.4′514—dc19   89–753
                                  CIP
                                  AC

Front cover: As the *Lusitania* sinks into the sea, passengers crowd the lifeboats to escape death.

Words that are printed in **bold** the first time they appear in the text are explained in the glossary.

Typeset by DP Press, Sevenoaks, Kent
Printed in Italy by G. Canale & C.S.p.A, Turin

CONTENTS

A SURVIVOR'S ACCOUNT

We had just finished lunch when the deafening explosion happened. My mother and father were still in the dining room, but I had been allowed to go up on deck to play soccer with some of the other children on board.

Just as one boy kicked the ball, there was a loud and terrifying noise. A massive fountain of water flew upward beside the ship. The whole vessel moved and I was knocked over. As I stood up, the ship began to tilt and alarms and bells started to sound.

Men and women came up on deck. Some of the sailors began working on the **lifeboats**. I wanted to be with my parents, but there were so many people that I could not find my way to the dining room. Instead, I stood beside the door to our cabin in the hope that they would find me there.

After a few minutes, the ship tilted again. Some people slipped overboard as they tried to get into the lifeboats. Several boats and rafts were lowered into the water, carrying some of the passengers to safety. There were still hundreds of people on deck, but my parents were nowhere to be seen.

Below *The explosion threw people to the deck. Passengers did not realize what had happened, until the order was given to abandon ship.*

Water poured into the shattered hull of the Lusitania so quickly that she began to sink before the first lifeboats could be launched.

Suddenly a man I did not know asked me what I was doing. I told him I was waiting for my parents. He said that they were not on board and that I ought to get off the ship. He picked me

Left *The upper decks of the Lusitania were lined with lifeboats. Unfortunately, few could be launched before the ship sank.*

Below *A French illustration showing some of the survivors. Some people remained in the water for hours before being rescued.*

As the horrified survivors watched from their lifeboats, the ship rose up from the water. After remaining still for a moment, the Lusitania *plunged beneath the waves.*

up and carried me to the rail of the deck. He shouted at a lifeboat in the water far beneath us. Then he threw me into the sea. One of the women in the boat pulled me on board. I was wet and very cold.

The boat was filled with men and women. A couple of sailors rowed the boat away from the ship. There were still a lot of people on the deck. Some of them leaped into the sea, while others stood still, waiting. Suddenly

the stern of the ship reared upward. Then the whole ship plunged beneath the waves. Several of the people in the boat began to cry. They said the people left behind must have died.

We drifted in the boat for quite a long time. Then a fishing boat came alongside. We all climbed aboard and were given hot tea to drink. I missed my mother, so I stayed close to the woman who had pulled me from the water into the lifeboat.

Our rescuers took us to a small town with a **jetty**. As I climbed ashore I saw my mother and father standing among the other survivors. I ran to them, feeling happy and relieved that they were still alive.

THE WORLD AT WAR

World War I, which began in August 1914, involved nearly every country in Europe. Germany, Austria – Hungary and their **allies** fought against Britain, France, Russia and their allies. Many non-European countries, like the United States and China, remained neutral at first.

During the first few weeks of the war it seemed as if Germany and its allies were winning. German troops marched deep into France and Russia. But then they were stopped, and land warfare became a virtual **stalemate**. Long lines of trenches ran across Europe. The soldiers fought from these trenches, protected by barbed wire and heavy **artillery**. Neither side was able to break through the defenses of the other.

So, when land warfare ground to a halt, the German leaders looked for another way to win the war. They knew that Britain depended on merchant shipping. Britain did not produce enough food to feed all its people, nor did it have enough **raw materials** to support its industry. Food, and such things as iron ore and ammunition, had to be bought abroad and shipped into Britain. The German leaders decided that if they could stop the merchant ships from reaching Britain, they would win the war.

At first, the German Navy relied on fast, heavily armed warships that sank British ships in the Pacific and Atlantic Oceans. However, the superior British Royal Navy sank or captured all these ships within a few months. The Germans then decided to use submarines, known as U-boats.

U-boats were able to lurk beneath the waves, completely out of sight. They could fire **torpedoes** at ships and then escape without being seen. Only ships with special equipment could track down submarines and destroy them. On January 1, 1915, a U-boat gained a great victory when it sank the British **battleship** *Formidable*. However, U-boats could travel only short distances. They could operate no farther afield than the North Sea, the English Channel and nearby areas of the Atlantic Ocean.

Left *The construction of trenches meant the war on land came to a halt. Thousands of men fought to gain a few miles of ground.*

Right *It was supplies such as these that enabled Britain to survive, and that the Germans attempted to sabotage.*

International laws, agreed to by many countries, govern warfare. One such law states that a merchant ship should not be sunk without warning. Any warship must first inform the merchant ship and then allow time for the merchant crew to take to lifeboats and escape.

However, the U-boat captains soon discovered a problem. If they gave warning of an attack, the merchant ships would have enough time to radio for help. Because they could only operate close to Britain, the U-boats found themselves threatened with attack from fast British warships.

Left A British merchant ship struck by a torpedo. Below A magazine illustration showing the interior of a German U-boat and its equipment.

2 PERISCOPES

DECK NAVIGATING STATION

ARMOURED CONNING TOWER

HIGH BOW TO KEEP DE DRY WHILE CRUISI ON SURFA

3 IN GUN STOWED

3 IN GUN BELOW

TORPEDO HATCH

TORPEDO ROOM

WIRELESS MASTS STOWED DOWN

TRIMMING TANK

NE OF STERN JBES ADED

CREW

TWIN SCREWS

STORAGE BATTERIES

ENGINE ROOM

OIL FUEL

INNER BALLAST TANKS

BATTERIES

TORPED ROOM WIT 2 TUBES LOAD & 4 SPARE TORPEDO

SPEED { 17 KNOTS SURFACE 10 KNOTS SUBMERGED

BALLAST TANKS FORMING SHOULDER OF OUTER HULL

OPERATING COMPARTMEN

Above *A U-boat, decorated for having made another victorious attack.*

Above *A U-boat sinks a fishing boat, then shoots the survivors.*

The German leaders therefore told their U-boat captains not to issue any warning at all. They pointed out that the laws had been drawn up before U-boats or fast surface craft had been invented. Germany stated it would be unfair to apply old-fashioned rules to a modern war.

On February 4, 1915, Admiral Von Pohl, Chief of the **Marine Staff** in Berlin, made the following official statement: "The waters around Great Britain and Ireland, including the whole of the English Channel, are herewith proclaimed a war region. On and after February 18, every enemy merchant vessel found in this war region will be destroyed, without its always being found possible to warn the crew or passengers of the dangers threatening." This meant that any British or French ship could be sunk on sight.

The number of merchant ships being sunk increased sharply. The British Navy took special measures against the U-boats. Heavily armed merchant ships, called Q-ships, patrolled the area, and 1,000 fast patrol craft were sent to sea. Under these circumstances, the U-boat captains became even more ruthless in their actions. The scene was set for the terrible tragedy of the *Lusitania*.

THE LUSITANIA SAILS

The passenger liner *Lusitania* left New York for Liverpool at 10:00 a.m. on Saturday, May 1, 1915. She was carrying 1,255 passengers and nearly 700 crew members. The ship was a magnificent floating palace, designed to carry passengers across the Atlantic Ocean. She had been launched in 1906 in Scotland, and was the pride of the Cunard Shipping Company.

The *Lusitania* was 788 feet (239 meters) long and weighed about 40,000 tons. As a liner, she had been designed to combine speed with comfort, and was capable of twenty-five **knots**. Her cabins were spacious and well equipped, and the dining rooms and kitchens were better than those of many hotels. She was therefore a popular ship with people who needed to make the otherwise uncomfortable Atlantic crossing.

Below *Large crowds waved goodbye as the* Lusitania *left New York. Few realized the dangers ahead.*

Right *A cross section of the* Lusitania *showing the impressive layout of this luxurious passenger liner.*

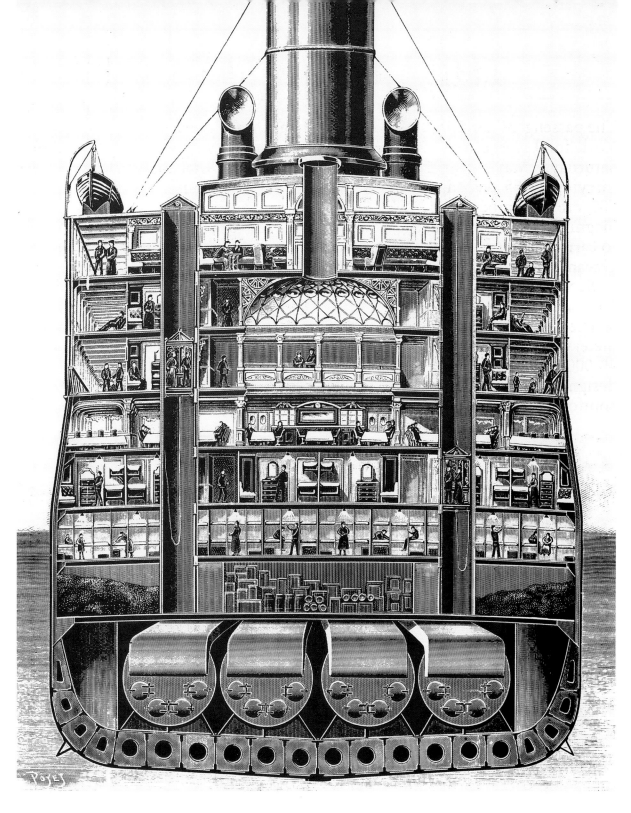

Left *The first-class lounge was furnished with the finest chairs and tables and roofed with stained-glass windows.*

Below *The captain's bridge, from which the entire ship was controlled.*

The *Lusitania* had completed several of her voyages since the start of World War I and had never run into any trouble. The passengers who booked cabins had no reason to feel worried. Liners did not carry ammunition or soldiers, so they were not military targets. It was widely thought that the U-boat campaign affected only ships carrying cargoes.

However, on April 22, the German Embassy in Washington released this statement to American newspapers: "In accordance with the notice given by the Imperial German Government, vessels flying the flags of Great Britain or any of her allies are liable to destruction; travelers sailing in ships of Great Britain do so at their own risk." Later, an anonymous telegram declared: "Have it on definite authority, *Lusitania* is to be torpedoed." However, because other warnings of this kind had been issued to similar ships before, and they had not been sunk, no less than 218 Americans ignored the message and sailed with the *Lusitania*.

When the liner left New York, it was commanded by Captain William Thomas Turner, an experienced and respected seaman. As the ship neared Britain, Turner ordered precautions against attack to be taken. The number of lookouts on duty was doubled; all interior watertight doors were locked shut, and the lifeboats were made ready for launching.

As the *Lusitania* approached Ireland, the British Navy radioed a special message to Captain Turner warning him that a German U-boat had been reported off the south coast of Ireland. The message also gave Captain Turner advice on which route to follow. Turner changed course accordingly, but unfortunately, the move was not enough to save his ship.

Right *Captain Turner who was in command of the* Lusitania.

Left *Passengers boarding the* Lusitania *at Liverpool. Special trains brought the passengers right to the dockside ready to climb aboard.*

TORPEDO!

The morning of May 7 dawned as the *Lusitania* steamed through dense fog off the southwest coast of Ireland. By noon, the weather had changed for the better. Warm sunshine bathed the *Lusitania* as it plowed through a calm sea. They were ideal conditions for the liner. Captain Turner reduced the ship's speed to eighteen knots so that the *Lusitania* would arrive in Liverpool at high tide.

The passengers went down to the dining rooms for lunch as the liner continued on course. They expected to arrive in Liverpool within a few hours. By 2:15 p.m. several passengers had finished their meals and were strolling on deck or resting in their cabins.

Below *The decks of the ship allowed children to play and adults to rest peacefully after lunch.*

The front page of a London newspaper that announced the tragedy the morning after the attack. Newspapers around the world were horrified by the attack on an unarmed passenger ship.

Captain Turner was on the **bridge** keeping a close eye on the progress of the ship.

Unseen by the Captain, or anyone else, U-boat 20 was lurking only a few hundred yards away. The U-boat lay slightly beneath the surface of the water with only its **periscope** showing. Its captain, Walter Schwieger, watched the approaching liner through the periscope. He had orders to sink every British ship he sighted. He took

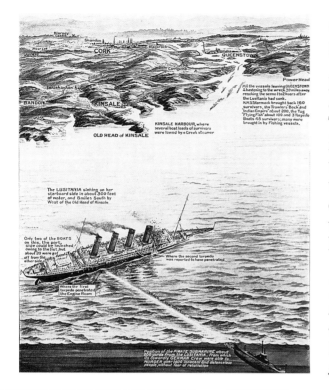

careful aim with his torpedoes and gave the order to fire.

On board the *Lusitania*, Leslie Morten, one of the lookout men, cried out, "There is a torpedo." Captain Turner rushed to the rail of the bridge in time to see the trails of two torpedoes. Both missiles slammed into the ship and exploded. A massive column of water and smoke flew upward. Turner felt the ship shudder. He knew immediately that the ship

Left *This map shows exactly where the Lusitania was sunk.*

Below *Captain Turner watches the fateful approach of the torpedoes.*

was going to sink. He first ordered the engines to switch to reverse and then gave the command to abandon ship.

The passengers and crew heard the alarms and came up on deck. They moved to their emergency positions without panic, but realized that something was terribly wrong. The torpedoes had struck the engine room and destroyed the engines. Without reverse it was impossible to stop the ship. The *Lusitania* was still moving forward at a speed of eighteen knots.

The enormous pressure this built up caused the watertight doors to burst open. The sea flooded through the length of the vessel. The *Lusitania* was sinking very quickly indeed. Even

Above *The first attempt to launch a lifeboat ended in disaster. The speed of the ship destroyed the boat.*

more dangerous was the fact that the high speed of the ship made it impossible to launch any lifeboats. One brave group of crew members volunteered to try. As soon as their boat reached the water it was overturned and smashed to pieces. Nobody could do anything but wait.

After about ten minutes the *Lusitania* slowed down. Another lifeboat was lowered. This time it stayed afloat. Soon, dozens of boats and rafts were being launched, but not all. The ship was tilting so badly that

Left Dozens of small craft rushed to help with the rescue. Fishing boats and naval gunboats were among the first on the scene. Their crews pulled many survivors from the water and carried them back to shore.

about half the lifeboats were trapped on board. Some four minutes after the first lifeboat got away, the ship lurched. The **bow** dived under water and the **stern** lifted high into the air.

Hundreds of people, unable to climb into lifeboats, crowded the decks. Captain Turner remained on the bridge, giving orders for the evacuation of the ship. Then he turned to his assistant saying, "You can go now and try to save yourself."

Poised at a steep angle, the ship shook. The few people who could find **lifebelts** leaped into the sea and hoped for the best. Others jumped and began to swim away. One mother who could not swim gave her baby to a man who could, hoping her child would be saved. Others knelt down to pray.

Then, in the words of one survivor, "With a lazy gliding motion, she slid out of sight without a sound, except the death gurgle of her boilers exploding under water. She left a terrible swirling **vortex** in which people were engulfed like flies." Captain Turner remained standing on the bridge as the ship went down, but he too managed to escape. He found himself swimming in a sea filled with dead bodies. Only eighteen minutes had passed since the torpedoes struck.

Captain Schwieger, who was in charge of the submarine that fired the torpedoes, watched the scene through his periscope. He made no attempt to help the survivors. He merely filled in a report and turned for home.

Both sides made use of the disaster in their publicity. Above An Irish poster encourages men to join the army. Left A medallion, *celebrating the German victory, mocks British anger at the sinking.*

21

THE RESCUE

As soon as the torpedoes struck, Captain Turner ordered an **SOS** message to be sent out. Naval vessels picked up the signal and altered course to help. Meanwhile the explosion had been heard by the lighthousekeeper on the Old Head of Kinsale, a promontory on the south coast of Ireland. He at once alerted the coastguard. Small craft put out from several ports in southern Ireland to join the rescue attempt. Immediate help came from a dozen fishing boats that happened to be nearby.

The fishing boats were the first to arrive. They dragged people from the water. As soon as each boat was full, it turned for the nearby port of Kinsale to drop off the survivors. The fishermen then put back to sea to collect more. The return journey took a long time. Some people remained in the water for as long as four hours. Many people could not survive for this amount of time. They died of exposure or drowned.

Survivors were given blankets, food and drink as they reached Kinsale.

Above *Local schoolchildren inspect the lifeboats that brought survivors ashore.*

Right *Two survivors of the disaster, photographed just minutes after reaching shore.*

Left *Two couples rescued from the wreck make their way to a tea shop in the streets of Queenstown.*

Left *Stranded passengers from the Lusitania waited in the streets of Queenstown for transportation to take them on the rest of their journey to England.*

A newspaper that showed some famous people who had been on board.

Most of the survivors were taken to Queenstown, about 15 miles (25 km) northeast of Kinsale, where they were given tea and food. Officials drew up a list of names of the survivors and the dead. Only then was it realized that a total of 1,198 people had been lost.

The dead bodies were laid out in the Market Hall at Queenstown. Relatives who had survived were then faced with the awful task of identifying the dead. Eventually, the survivors continued their journey to Liverpool on other ships.

THE ANGRY AFTERMATH

The terrible news of the *Lusitania* disaster had a profound effect on all those who heard it. People were upset, angry and determined on revenge. The first inkling of the tragedy reached London and New York by radio at about 5:00 p.m. on the day of the torpedo attack. At first, no details were known; only that the ship had been attacked. By 6:30 p.m. it was known that the ship had sunk.

Large crowds gathered outside the offices of the Cunard Shipping Company in London, Liverpool and New York. Everybody was anxious for news. They wanted to know how many people had died, and if their friends and relatives had survived. In New York, a passing German spoke up. He shouted, "We warned them. Our embassy advertised the warning." The crowd attacked him, and only prompt action by the police saved him.

In Liverpool, where most of the crew lived, the crowd was even more angry. Shops and businesses owned by

Below *As soon as news of the disaster arrived, crowds gathered outside the Cunard Company offices.*

Left *A German postcard celebrating the sinking of the Lusitania. Such objects infuriated the United States and Britain.*

Below left *An illustration showing a diver inspecting the wreck.*

German **immigrants** were attacked and burned. The police had to turn out in force to stop the riot.

A few days after the sinking an official inquiry began. The details revealed shocked the world. Merchant ships carrying ammunition might be targets for attack, but not liners with innocent civilians on board. In the United States, the news that 139 Americans had died made the public particularly angry. When Captain Turner was asked if he had received any warning from the German submarine, he said simply, "None whatever. Straight done and finished."

It appeared that Germany had deliberately broken the laws of war. Many people in the United States expected President Wilson to declare war on Germany. Instead, he said that

Above *A poster that encouraged men to join the U.S. Army by appealing to their sense of history.*

Above *A portrait of Woodrow Wilson, President of the United States at the time of the disaster. It was due to Wilson that Germany called off its U-boat attacks soon afterward.*

the United States must set an example of peace and not fight. "There was such a thing as a nation being so right that it did not need to convince others by force that it was right."

The behavior of the German government over the affair quickly inflamed American opinion even more. It stated that some ammunition

had been on board the *Lusitania*, which made her a legitimate target. It was also said that if the liner's crew had spotted the submarine, they would have notified the British Navy. When it became known that Germany had had a medal made to commemorate the sinking of the *Lusitania*, calls for the United States to enter the

submarine attacks. However, on February 1, 1917, Germany began U-boat attacks once again. Merchant ships were sunk without warning, and several Americans were killed. The horror of the *Lusitania* was still fresh in the memories of the world and, on April 6, the United States declared war on Germany and its allies. The *Lusitania* was to be avenged.

Below *This combination of photograph and illustration commemorates those who died during World War I.*

Above *A poster imagining President Wilson dreaming of catching German U-boats. The United States finally declared war on Germany and its allies on April 6, 1917. Before then, many Americans had volunteered to join the British Army, partly in revenge for the attack on the* Lusitania.

war increased. Many Americans volunteered for the British Army.

President Wilson still refused to declare war. Instead, he sent strong and angry messages to Germany. These caused Germany to call off the

GLOSSARY

Allies   Nations that join together against a common enemy.

Artillery   Large guns on wheels, often operated from trenches during wartime.

Battleship   The largest and most powerful type of warship; it carries many guns.

Bow   The front end of a boat or ship.

Bridge   The raised area above the deck of a ship from which the captain gives his orders.

Immigrants   People who come to live and settle in a new country.

Jetty   A long, thin platform that juts out into the sea, to which boats or ships can be tied.

Knots   A measure of speed, used by ships. One knot is equal to 1.15 miles (1.85 km) per hour.

Lifebelts   Rings of buoyant material that can be worn as belts and will keep a person afloat.

Lifeboats   Small boats carried by large ships in which crew and passengers can escape if the ship is in danger of sinking.

Marine Staff   The most important admirals in Germany who decided what action the navy should take in wartime.

Periscope   A tube with a lens through which a submarine captain can see above the water without surfacing his craft.

Raw materials   Natural materials, such as iron ore, coal and oil, that are taken from the earth to be used in industry.

SOS   The international distress signal.

Stalemate   A position in war or a game, in which movement is impossible and neither side can win.

Stern   The back end of a boat or ship.

Torpedoes   Underwater missiles fired by submarines and ships, which can sink a ship.

Vortex   A whirling mass of water, such as the spiraling movement of water around a whirlpool.

FURTHER READING

The First World War by John Pimlott, Franklin Watts, 1986
See Inside a Submarine by Jonathan Rutland, Warwick, 1988
Ships and Other Seacraft by Brian Williams, Warwick, 1984
Ships and Submarines by Michael Grey, Franklin Watts, 1986
Submarines by Richard Humblo, Franklin Watts, 1985
Submarines by C.J. Norman, Franklin Watts, 1986

ACKNOWLEDGMENTS

The publishers would like to thank the following for providing the photographs in this book: BBC Hulton 6 (top), 9, 10 (top), 11 (left), 16, 21 (bottom), 23 (bottom), 24 (top), 24 (bottom), 25, 26, 27 (top), 29 (bottom); ET Archive 6 (bottom), 8, 27 (bottom), 28 (left); John Frost 14 (top), 14 (bottom), 15 (left), 15 (right), 17; The Mansell Collection 23 (top), 28 (right); Mary Evans cover, 5, 10 (bottom), 11 (right), 13, 18, 20, 29 (top); Peter Newark's Military Pictures 21 (top). The illustrations on pages 5, 7, 12, 18, 19 and 22 are by Nik Spender.

INDEX